Animal Fun Facts

FUN FACTS ABOUT SNAKES

by Julie Murray

Dash!
LEVELED READERS
2

An Imprint of Abdo Zoom • abdobooks.com

Dash!
LEVELED READERS

Level 1 – Beginning
Short and simple sentences with familiar words or patterns for children who are beginning to understand how letters and sounds go together.

Level 2 – Emerging
Longer words and sentences with more complex language patterns for readers who are practicing common words and letter sounds.

Level 3 – Transitional
More developed language and vocabulary for readers who are becoming more independent.

THIS BOOK CONTAINS RECYCLED MATERIALS

abdobooks.com

Published by Abdo Zoom, a division of ABDO, PO Box 398166, Minneapolis, Minnesota 55439.

Printed in the United States of America, North Mankato, Minnesota.
052021
092021

Photo Credits: Alamy, iStock, Science Source, Shutterstock, ©Blair Hedges, Penn State p18
Production Contributors: Kenny Abdo, Jennie Forsberg, Grace Hansen, John Hansen
Design Contributors: Candice Keimig, Neil Klinepier

Library of Congress Control Number: 2020919494

Publisher's Cataloging in Publication Data

Names: Murray, Julie, author.
Title: Fun facts about snakes / by Julie Murray
Description: Minneapolis, Minnesota : Abdo Zoom, 2022 | Series: Animal fun facts | Includes online resources and index.
Identifiers: ISBN 9781098224493 (lib. bdg.) | ISBN 9781098225438 (ebook) | ISBN 9781098225902 (Read-to-Me ebook)
Subjects: LCSH: Snakes--Juvenile literature. | Snakes--Behavior--Juvenile literature. | Reptiles--Behavior--Juvenile literature. | Questions and answers--Juvenile literature. | Animal behavior--Juvenile literature.
Classification: DDC 597.96--dc23

Table of Contents

Fun Facts About Snakes

There are more than 3,000 kinds of snakes. The black mamba is the fastest. It can move up to 12 miles per hour (20 km/h)!

There are 600 kinds of **venomous** snakes. The inland taipan has the most toxic venom of all.

Its venom can kill a human
in 45 minutes!

There are five kinds of flying snakes. These snakes glide through the air. The paradise tree snake can "fly" nearly 330 feet (100 m).

All snakes **shed** their skin. Young snakes may shed every few weeks. Adults shed around two to four times a year.

Snakes eat their food whole. They can eat animals much larger than themselves. A python has been known to eat a cow!

The **decapitated** head of a dead snake can still bite! This is because its **reflexes** are still working.

A snake smells with its tongue. It has a special **organ** inside its mouth. This allows the snake to "taste" a scent.

The Barbados threadsnake is the smallest snake. It is only 4 inches (10 cm) long. It looks like an earthworm.

The green anaconda is the largest snake. It can be 30 feet (9 m) long. It can weigh over 500 pounds (227 kg)!

Animal Spotlight

King Cobra

Size: Up to 18 feet (5.5 m) long; Up to 20 pounds (9 kg)

Appearance: green, brown, or black in color with markings; pale yellow neck that can flatten and fan out

Range: mainly India, southern China, and Southeast Asia

Habitat: forests, mangrove swamps, and plains

Diet: other snakes, lizards, eggs, small mammals

Lifespan: 20 years

Glossary

decapitated – to have the head cut off of.

organ – a part of an animal that performs a particular task. The heart, lungs, and skin are all organs.

reflex – a response or reaction by the body.

shed – to cast off or take off.

venomous – making a fluid, called venom, that is poison to humans and animals. A venomous animal makes venom that it can put into another animal with its bite or sting.

Index

Online Resources

Booklinks
NONFICTION NETWORK
FREE! ONLINE NONFICTION RESOURCES

To learn more about snakes, please visit **abdobooklinks.com** or scan this QR code. These links are routinely monitored and updated to provide the most current information available.